Nursery Rhymes for Modern Times

Volume I: Great Americans

◇◇◇◇

Philo F. Willetts, Jr.

Author

Nursery Rhymes for Modern Times
Volume I: Great Americans

ISBN 978-1-7327283-0-1

Library of Congress Control Number:2019905796

Cover and illustrations by Iva Sashiva
Book design by Stephen Schwartz

PHIDACTIC
PUBLISHING
WESTERLY, RI

Dedicated to my beloved grandchildren:

Henry, Grace, Avery, Ethan, and Nika
wishing you many years of enjoyable learning over long, healthy, and happy lives.

Table of Contents

Introduction

Recommended Audience: The educational rhymes contained herein are meant to be read to children: from infancy into elementary school.

The Advantage of Rhymes: Rhymes can entertain, and rhymes can educate. Importantly, our brains are "wired" to remember rhymes. The rhymes in this book can prime a lifetime of learning. This volume may help our children recognize and learn a little about some great people who made our nation and culture what it is. So they may be better prepared to learn more about them and excel in school. These verses can make more memorable the achievements and the personal qualities — benevolence, civility, diligence, fairness, honesty, perseverance, practice, and self-teaching — of some of our greatest people.

How to Use This Book: Parents, caregivers, and teachers might select just one of this book's rhymes to read to their children each day — before going onto the child's other favorite stories.

- Repeat the subject's name while viewing the picture. Practice and repeat recall: of names, faces, facts, and events. Quiz children to recall and name the people illustrated. Look for and allow children to identify other images of the same subjects: on currency, online, and elsewhere. Encourage children to try to make sense of what they see in the illustrations and hear in the verse. Praise each child for effort as well as achievement.

- Consider using the Teachable Moment section following each verse. Discuss the person and the times.

- Ask, encourage and be sure to respect all questions. Show children how we find credible information. Teach children the essential importance of teaching themselves.

- Consider doing the book's suggested activities, or create your own activities — to help children understand the people, the circumstances, and the issues they faced.

- Encourage children to learn and recite a few of the verse lines that encapsulate the subjects' key achievements. Memorizing two or more lines can not only lock in the facts contained, but also strengthen an important brain skill. And allow us to recognize and praise the child for the achievement.

Summary: This book may entertain small children through parental reading of word sounds and through the colorful illustrations. It will teach older children by discussion of the facts and issues contained. I hope that those who read these rhymes to our children may themselves choose to learn a little more about these and other great people. And help educate the next generation.

Philo F. Willetts, Jr.
Westerly, Rhode Island, April 2019

Benjamin Franklin
1706-1790

Benjamin Franklin left his father and mother,
To learn how to print from his older brother.
He quickly learned about printing machines;
He printed papers, books, and magazines.

He invented lightning rods and bifocal glasses;
He built elementary schools and college classes.
His Franklin Stove kept us warm at night.
He even found money for our freedom fight.

He helped our new nation win our first war.
He printed, invented, and did a lot more.
Ben was early to bed and early to rise.
Benjamin Franklin grew wealthy and wise.

Teachable Moment

Information:
Benjamin Franklin was apprenticed to his older brother, to learn the printing business. He also became a writer, a postmaster, an ambassador to France, a scientist, and many other things. He discovered that lightning was electricity. When in his 80's Franklin was the oldest member of the U.S. Constitutional Convention. And he made some good suggestions as to what rules our country should follow.

Franklin wrote and printed many things. He wrote Poor Richard's Almanac. He wrote funny stories — stories that made people laugh but that also taught people things. Before there were computer printers, printing presses were the only way to make multiple copies of writing, without having to write everything by hand. (See Alexander Hamilton and Abigail Adams following.)

Questions:
1. How can we tell that Benjamin Franklin lived in earlier times?
   [Hint: Different types of hat, clothes and shoes; a wood burning stove for heating; wearing of warmer clothing inside in winter; an old type of printing press before there were computer printers; and an old kind of wide board wooden floor.]

2. Would you have liked to have lived long ago? What would have been different then? Hint: No toilets, no iPads, no telephones, no TVs, no washing machines, etc.

3. Think of other questions to ask. And encourage children to ask questions.

Discussion:
Name the objects in this illustration. Guess their uses, and how they worked? Think of other activities such as costumes, role play, museum visits, or other activities to allow children to experience what it was like to live in the 18th century.

Thomas Jefferson
1743-1826

Thomas Jefferson said we were free
And we had rights to Life and Liberty.
On the 4th of July in 17 76
He said all men were equal in politics.

But his claim on the 4th of July
Made many later ask why
If all were equal, and life were fair,
They weren't so equal — anywhere.

President Jefferson bought us all a huge piece of land
The Louisiana Purchase let our nation expand
To the Rocky Mountains and Montana sky
At two cents an acre, a really great buy.

Teachable Moment

Information:
Thomas Jefferson wrote most of the Declaration of Independence, announced on the 4th of July 1776, telling the world that our nation was free and telling the world why our people wanted to be free.

Jefferson also said that all men were created equal. But, at that time many people, including women, African Americans, and Native American people were not allowed to be equal. Even Thomas Jefferson himself owned slaves. That wasn't fair. Several great Americans did much to change all that, as will be described later in this book.

Later, when he was president, Thomas Jefferson bought the Louisiana Territory from France in 1803. This more than 800,000 square mile land purchase greatly expanded the size of the United States. And Americans continued to push westward toward the Pacific Ocean, to settle our expanding country. Now fifteen states occupy the original Louisiana Purchase.

Questions:
1. What is Thomas Jefferson holding? [The Declaration of Independence that he substantially wrote.]

2. Were all people equal after Jefferson said they were?

Discussion:
Find where on the United States map is the Louisiana Purchase? Where are the Rocky Mountains? Where is the Atlantic Ocean? The Pacific Ocean? Canada? Where do we live? Show where the United States is located on a globe.

Louisiana
Territory

President George Washington 1732-1799

George Washington was an honest guy.
He didn't cheat, and he didn't lie.
When his father said, "Tell the truth to me."
George confessed, "I chopped down the cherry tree."

He always tried to do what's right.
He led the revolution fight
That forever set America free.
To his character we all agree.

President Washington was our country's guide.
He could have been king, but he stepped aside.
He's the father of our baby nation.
He forever earned our admiration.

Teachable Moment

Information:
George Washington was revered by Americans during his lifetime and for many decades after he died. Washington was honest. He had great character. He took great care to conduct himself properly. He led by example. He was tenacious and determined in his leadership of our revolutionary armies. Determination means to keep trying instead of quitting when things don't go well at first.

After unanimously elected our first president by the electoral college, he then set an example of being honest, fair, and doing what he thought was best for our country. He avoided acting like fancy or snobbish kings or rulers of other countries.

People would have allowed Washington to keep ruling and many would have allowed him to be a king. But, after two terms as president, Washington deliberately stepped aside, so that our country could elect a new ruler. When his old opponent, King George III of England heard that he reportedly said, If Washington stepped aside, "he is the greatest man alive."

Questions:
1. Why is George Washington called the father of our country?

2. Why is it so important to be honest, when you are dealing with other people?

Discussion:
Discuss why it is important to be determined when you must accomplish something important. And why is it important to be determined and to continue to try when things become difficult instead of quitting? Look up images of Washington on the internet. See the common Gilbert Stuart painted images that show Washington looking grim. Look also for the life bust done by the French artist, Hodon, showing Washington much more accurately as a strong, handsome man.

Alexander Hamilton
1757-1804

Alexander Hamilton lived long ago,
He wanted to learn; he wanted to know.
He studied hard when he was just a boy.
He said learning was better than any toy.

He wrote with a goose feather quill
And hoped that the ink didn't spill.
There were no computer printers then.
If he wanted a copy, he had to write it again.

When asked to handle our nation's money
What Hamilton learned wasn't so funny.
Hamilton found out, and then he showed
We broke our promise to pay what we owed.

Hamilton wrote and spoke and got all to know
That we must always pay back all that we owe.
That we must work and earn and save
And that to break a promise is to misbehave.

Teachable Moment

Information:
Hamilton, whenever he wanted to know more about something, would get several books and then would read about it. He taught himself what he needed to know.

Some countries and people who had previously loaned our country money had stopped trusting us, because we were not paying back the money we had borrowed. So Hamilton got the United States government pay the debts of the several states, when those states weren't paying what they owed. After Hamilton got our country to pay our debts, other countries started trusting us again.

Hamilton also established banks and a stock market, so people could save, borrow, or invest money to build businesses. This provided the money so that people could build factories, railroads, steamboats, and other businesses that built our country.

Questions:
1. Why did Hamilton use a large bird feather, a quill, to do his writing? Hint: There were no ink pens, electronic tablets, computers, or voice dictation systems for writing in Hamilton's time.

2. Why did Hamilton have to teach himself about some things? Answer: Because teachers cannot teach us every single thing that we need to know. Teachers can guide us. Teachers can teach us how to read, how to think clearly, and how to teach ourselves. All children should know that they must occasionally teach themselves and know how to do so.

Discussion:
Get a goose feather quill and a small cup of watercolor or other washable paint and practice writing or drawing with them. Then make another copy to see how cumbersome it is to have to make duplicate copies in this manner. To make multiple copies, Hamilton either had to write the whole thing again and again, or he had to go to printers, like Ben Franklin. The printer would read Hamilton's handwriting, then set up individual type letters into words and sentences, and then print copies. Discuss how we can make copies of papers today. Now we have copiers, printers, and digital cameras.

Abigail Adams
1744-1818

Abigail Adams was President Adams' wife.
She gave her family a better life.
She helped her husband better rule.
She helped her son do well in school.

She wrote letters with a feather quill.
And, when the sun set under the window sill
She wrote at night by candlelight.
She lived long before the electric light.

Abigail died of typhoid fever
But we wouldn't have had to grieve her
If she had only got
A vaccination shot.

Teachable Moment

Information:
Abigail Adams' husband, President John Adams, was very smart. But he sometimes was grumpy and unpleasant to people. And some people made fun of him, because he ate too much, didn't exercise, and became obese. Some people called President Adams, "his rotundity."

So Abigail talked to and advised her husband. She helped President Adams be a nicer person and be a better president. See how Abigail Adams also used a quill instead of a pen? There were no emails then. So, people wrote lots of letters to each other. And there were no electric lights then. So, if were dark outside, Abigail Adams would use candles to get enough light to write her letters.

Abigail Adams got sick and then died of a disease called typhoid in 1818. Now, people get vaccination shots, so they don't have to worry about getting sick or dying from typhoid fever.

Abigail and John Adams had a son named John Quincy Adams. John Quincy Adams was smart. He spoke six different languages. And John Quincy Adams later became president, too, in 1825. In this illustration Abigail Adams is writing to her son, Quincy.

Questions:
1. Why did Abigail Adams have to write letters to get messages to her family and friends?

2. Did it take very long for a letter to get from one person to another? Why? [Horseback, stagecoach, walking were the slow means of transport then. No telephones, internet, then.]

Discussion:
Think of all the ways that we now can get messages to other people, faster than Abigail Adams could?

14

Chief Justice John Marshall 1755-1835

Justice John Marshall read long legal briefs;
He was the greatest of our Supreme Court chiefs.
He decided who's right, and he knew who lied.
We lost a great judge when John Marshall died.

In Marbury v. Madison in 1803
His carefully written Court decree
Said that his Court decided the law.
The greatest decision we ever saw.

Teachable Moment

Information:
John Marshall established that the U.S. Supreme Court decided the law. He said that the Supreme Court decided whether a law was constitutional and could be enforced or was not in keeping with the Constitution and should be thrown out.

Justice Marshall cleverly decided the famous Marbury v Madison case of 1803 to keep each side satisfied, while establishing that the U.S. Supreme Court could throw out a law of Congress, if that law violated the U.S. Constitution. After that, everyone knew that the Constitution was the ultimate law, and the U.S. Supreme Court was the final judge of what the laws were.

Children who remember this 1803 Marbury v. Madison case and the date will be primed to learn more when they later hear about the case in school.

John Marshall's Supreme Court decided many other important cases during the 34 years that he sat on the Court.

Questions:
1. Do you think that there were computers and printers to write with in John Marshall's time? How can you tell by this picture? Note the quill pen and the ink well needed to write anything, because there were no computers or computer printers then.

2. What does the phrase: Equal Justice Under the Law, engraved on the U.S. Supreme Court building, mean?
(See Ruth Bader Ginsburg in Elizabeth Cady Stanton later in this book.)

Activities:
Discuss why we sometimes need courts to decide who's right, or to decide who owns something. And why we need rules and laws. If there were no courts, could the strongest or meanest person always get to grab things that he wanted? Would we always live in fear that no one would protect our rights to own our houses, toys, and other things?

Consider having a simple mock court, to decide who owns a valuable toy or iPhone. Have people argue — civilly and courteously — why they and not the other should own the toy. Discuss why quiet proof, honest witnesses, and other good evidence of ownership are much more important than loud, but unsupported, declarations, claims, and assertions. Choose a smaller person to be the one with the better evidence, showing how a weaker person can win in

Dolley Madison
1768-1849

Dolley Madison was one of a few
She was nice to all she knew.
As President Madison's wife,
She gave all a more pleasant life.

She made enemies like one another,
By inviting those who hated each other
To eat at the Madison's table,
And be as nice as they were able.

She planned her table's seatings,
So all had friendly meetings.
Her dinners weren't just for fun.
She got important agreements done.

Teachable Moment

Information:
Dolley Madison showed how, by getting people who disagreed with each other to socialize, they could get to know and often like each other. She invited them to her dinners and made everyone feel good about themselves and about the others at the table. She politely made them behave. Then these Congressmen would start working together to do what was best for all, instead of just attacking or being mean to each other. Some said that Dolley Madison got more agreements done in an evening than happened in a week of President Madison's meetings.

Many people would like to see our current leaders be nicer to each other now, so they can work together more effectively. Dolley Madison set an excellent example of how to do so, a long time ago.

Important Point: When you are mean to people, they won't want to listen to you or hear what you say. Even if you are right, they won't want to hear it, if you are mean to them. So, it is important to be polite and nice to people — especially if you want them to agree with what you think and believe or do what you want them to do.

Questions:
1. Why is it important to be polite and nice to other people, especially the people with whom we disagree?

2. When a person is mean to another person, will other people listen to him? And will other people want to do what a mean person wants them to do?

Activities: Try to name or act out all the ways that people can be rude when talking to each other. And how to avoid doing those things. Hint: Yelling, saying unkind things, laughing at the other, making fun of the other, interrupting the other person, ignoring the other person, not listening to the other person, not answering the other person, lying, having an unpleasant facial or body language expression, etc.

Describe how you feel if someone does these things to you? How do you think other people feel when done to them?

Sequoyah
about 1775-1843

Sequoyah was a Native Cherokee
From North Carolina and Tennessee.
He taught his people how to write with ease,
With lots more letters than the a b c's.

The Cherokee felt President Jackson's hate.
On that terrible date — eighteen thirty-eight.
They still remember, after all these years,
When they were forced to the West on the Trail of Tears.

Teachable Moment

Information:
Sequoyah's Cherokee people had no written language. They just had a spoken language. Sequoyah invented a written language for his people. English has just 26 letters, and the same letters sometimes sound differently at different times. Sequoyah's language was better than English, because he included 86 letters. Each letter was a different sound in the spoken Cherokee language. So people could learn how to read and write Cherokee much more easily than learning English. As soon as they had a written language, the Cherokee wrote books and newspapers.

When people can write about events and about their ideas, then, so long as the writings are saved, everyone else can read and learn about them. Writing is like everyone shares a giant brain. Without writing, people would have to remember everything that they were ever told — inside their own heads. And often memories fade, change, or disappear over time or when a person goes away. So, writing makes our total, combined human memory much greater.

Trail of Tears:
President Jackson sometimes got mad at people for no good reason. He got mad at the Cherokee people and made them leave their homes in the east and go to some new lands out in the west of our country. This wasn't fair. The Cherokee remember this as The Trail of Tears, because some people cried when they were made to leave their homes.

Questions:
1. Did all Native Americans wear big feather headdresses? No. (See Sitting Bull later.) Different peoples dressed differently. Sequoyah often is pictured wearing a cloth turban for a hat.

2. Why is it important for you and for everyone else to learn how to write?

3. How would you feel if you were forced to leave your home, have to leave some of your stuff, and then move to a place far away, when you didn't want to? Would that be fair?

Activities:
The map shows the trail over which the Cherokee were forced to march in 1838. Can you use your finger to trace the red dotted Trail of Tears? Can you find North Carolina, where the march began and Oklahoma, where the march ended? Obtain some alphabet letters from an art store. Take the letters: P, A, and T. Show how the letters sound in the word, "pat," or in the word, "tap." Or S, P, O, and T. (spot and tops.) Do the same with other letters, so children can understand how letters often represent sounds and we often can make sense of words by knowing those sounds.

Samuel F. B. Morse
1791-1872

Samuel Morse rode his own horse
And the news was slower by half.
So, he invented a special code of course;
He brought us the telegraph.

Telegraph wires were so much better.
Now dashes and dots could easily compress
Then send numbers, notes, and even a letter
A thousand times faster than the Pony Express.

Teachable Moment

Information:
Long ago, there were no cars and no trucks. And, until 1869, there were no trains that traveled all the way across our country. Horse-pulled stagecoaches were slow. As Americans continued to move toward the western part of our country, they found that sending messages back and forth was slow and difficult. Before the telegraph, the Pony Express was the fastest way to get a letter across the western part of our country.

Young men put letters into horse saddlebags and rode fast. When a horse got tired, the rider would stop at the next Pony Express station and then jump onto another, well-rested horse to carry the mail to the next station. By using several horses and riders, the Pony Express could carry letters across the country in just a few days.

The Pony Express was much faster than stagecoaches had been before. But Samuel Morse's telegraph wire was much faster still. Telegraph wires could carry an electric message across the same distance in a few minutes. So the Pony Express was no longer necessary and it stopped after a few years.

See Samuel Morse's telegraph key that allowed operators to click groups of dots and dashes (short and long clicks)? Telegraph operators knew what alphabet letters these clicks meant. They called this system Morse Code.

Questions:
1. Before there were telegraph machines and wires, how could a person get a message to another person?

2. Now how many ways are there to get our message to someone else?

Activities:
Learn the Morse code for some letters. Write down or print out the letters and the Morse code dot and dash equivalents. Then divide children and have them send messages to each other, using only the code. So they must translate words into code to send. And translate code into words when received. A quick tap will be a dot. A tap with a slight pause will be a dash.
Teach children the Morse code international SOS [Save Our Ship] and that it means "Help." Morse Code for S is dot, dot, dot. Code for O is dash, dash, dash. Code for S is dot, dot, dot. So SOS is dot, dot, dot followed by dash, dash, dash, followed by dot, dot, dot.

Set up a Pony Express system in a group of children, with messages relayed across a distance.

Frederick Douglass
1818-1895

Frederick Douglass, an unhappy slave,
Would often fight and misbehave.
He tried and tried 'til he could flee
And make himself completely free.

He angrily said that slaves weren't free.
Every 4th of July he would disagree.
He said "all men are equal" was just a lie,
He wrote: What to a Slave is the Fourth of July?

He asked why should slaves celebrate
A 4th of July freedom date,
When their country would not agree
To set its slaves forever free?

Teachable Moment

Information:
Slaves were people who were owned by other people. Most had originally been made to come from Africa against their will. They couldn't leave their owners or do what they wanted. They had to work for their owners for no money. They had no rights. If they ran away and were caught, they could be punished. That wasn't fair.

Frederick Douglass was a born as a slave, but he hated being a slave. He finally was able to run away, and he moved to the north part of the United States, where African Americans could then be free.

Frederick Douglass learned how to read, and he practiced how to write really well. Then he wrote and printed a newspaper called The North Star. He was still angry about having been a slave. He used his newspaper to tell people to free all the slaves.

Frederick Douglass also visited and became a friend to President Lincoln. Douglass taught Lincoln about what African Americans thought, wanted, and needed.

There now are very few slaves left in the world. Owning slaves in America is not allowed and is against the law because of President Abraham Lincoln.

Questions:
1. Jefferson said all men were created equal. But, was everyone equal then? Is everyone equal now? Is life now fair for everyone?

2. How are things different now compared to when Frederick Douglass lived?

Activities:
Find on the world map or globe where African slaves came from and how they were carried by ships across the ocean to our country.
Discuss what a slave's life was like compared to the life of someone else who was free. What could or couldn't a slave

THE NORTH STAR.

what to a slave is the 4th of July?

Harriet Beecher Stowe 1811-1896

The famous Harriet Beecher Stowe
Wrote about slavery years ago.
She said that slaves weren't treated fair.
She made her readers start to care.

Stories can make us happy or sad.
Harriet's book made everyone mad.
Harriet Beecher Stowe was responsible for
Pushing us toward a great civil war.

Teachable Moment

Information:
Harriet Beecher Stowe wrote a book that said how people who were slaves were unhappy and were not treated very nice by the people who owned them. The people of the North started hating the people who owned slaves. But the people in the South who owned slaves hated what that book said about them.

Harriet Beecher Stowe's book, Uncle Tom's Cabin, made slave-owning people of the south and antislavery people of the north hate each other even more.

Later, during the Civil War, when President Lincoln met Harriet Beecher Stowe, he reportedly said, "So you're the little lady who caused this great big war!"

Questions:
1. Which can be more powerful, a written book or a weapon like a sword or gun?

2. What does it mean when people say, "The pen is mightier than the sword?"

3. Can somebody's writing something change other people's minds and get them to believe or do something new?

4. Which is more likely to change a person's mind about something: a.) Just tell a person what to think or believe?, or b.) Tell a story to make the person care about your idea and to show the other person why you are right? Hint: Many people don't like being told what to think. Most people like to hear stories. Our brains learn and respond better to stories than to just being told something. So, if you can tell a story about the harmful effect of something, a person will remember that better than just being told something is harmful.

5. Why is it important to learn how to speak and write well?

Activities:
Think about writing a book or a story to persuade people be better or to fix or improve something? Describe what you

President Abraham Lincoln 1809-1865

Honest Abe Lincoln was a poor little boy.
Often without shoes or even a toy.
His father made him work for free,
But Lincoln dreamed of what he could be.

He only had a year of school.
He learned rhetoric, and how to rule.
He taught himself what he needed to know
By day and night, by firelight, long ago.

He lost a brother, sister, and his mother.
He lost one son and then lost another.
He'd lost Ann Rutledge, his first true love.
But he never gave up; he rose above.

With malice toward none, he was often sad.
He was the best president we ever had.
He saved our nation in the Civil War,
And freed the slaves — for evermore.

Teachable Moment

Information:
Abraham Lincoln's two major achievements were:

• **Lincoln saved our country, the United States union** — preventing it from splitting into smaller countries — so we became a strong country that has been a major influence upon world events since then, and

• **Lincoln freed four million slaves** — by the Emancipation Proclamation of January 1, 1863, then later by getting the 13th Amendment through Congress toward state ratification in 1865.

Abraham Lincoln also showed how a poor person could achieve great things in America. Despite his lack of formal schooling, Lincoln loved to read. He always tried his best to understand whatever he read and what he heard people say. Then he would put those ideas into simple, understandable words. Importantly, Lincoln taught himself. Lincoln taught himself to be excellent at rhetoric. Rhetoric is about how to get other people to agree with what you think or what you want. To be good at rhetoric, you must have **Ethos:** be honest, so people will believe you, and be nice, so people will want to believe you. Use **Logos:** Use logical facts and provable arguments, so people will understand why you are right. And **Pathos:** You must use words and stories well, to connect emotionally with people, so they will understand, care about, and remember what you say.

Lincoln was honest and nice to people, so people listened to him and trusted him. And he used words logically and better than any other president. So he got people who didn't care, to start to care. He inspired people to fight to save the country — and to free the slaves.

Lincoln's first true love, Ann Rutledge, like Lincoln's son, Willie, and Abigail Adams, all died of typhoid in an age before there were typhoid vaccinations. Lincoln, whose little brother, older sister, and mother had also died, was devastated. Lincoln was often sad and depressed during his hard life.

Questions:
1. What were the two greatest things that Abraham Lincoln did?

Activities:
Describe how you, like Lincoln, can learn about things, if you have no teacher nearby or if you have no school to go to. Discuss the three basic components of rhetoric — ethos, logos, and pathos — and why having and using each is so

Ulysses S. Grant
1822-1885

General Grant led with care.
He brought his troops to where
The fighting would begin.
He always fought to win.

Ulysses Grant did his task.
No one ever had to ask
If U. S. Grant did his bit.
He never ever thought to quit.

He would never boast and never brag.
He just pushed the Union Army flag.
He was never rude, was never mean.
He led Lincoln's Civil War machine.

When Grant won the Civil War,
He lined up his army corps,
To salute the defeated Southern men
To show that we should all be friends again.

Teachable Moment

Information:
Ulysses Grant became the leading Union general of the Civil War. He carefully planned battles and wrote detailed instructions to his junior generals. So his soldiers knew what they were supposed to do. Grant won almost all of his battles, because he planned and led properly. And because he would not quit.

Other generals used to say mean things about each other and sometimes say mean things about President Lincoln. And other generals often made excuses about why they couldn't fight or why they lost battles. But US Grant did not make excuses. And he did not brag or say bad things about his rivals. Nobody likes people who are mean to other people, or who brag, or make excuses.

When Grant's armies finally won the Civil War, Grant had his soldiers stand up at attention and salute the Confederate soldiers that they had defeated — to show respect to their former enemy and to welcome them back to the Union. This was a highly unusual and gracious act.

Later, US Grant was elected president. He was fair to the defeated South. And he tried to be fair to Native-Americans. He even appointed a Native-American to his cabinet to help him rule.

Questions:
1. Do you like a person who brags? Or who says bad things about other people? Or makes excuses? What would other people think of you, if you were to act that way?

2. Why did Grant win most of his battles?

Activities:
Discuss why saluting the defeated enemy soldiers was a good and wise thing to do. If you win against other people, should you gloat, brag, or make fun of them? How would that make them feel? Wouldn't your opponent be less likely to hate you and more likely to get along with you, if you show kindness and respect after winning?

Elizabeth Cady Stanton 1815-1902

Elizabeth Cady Stanton set her sights
On getting women's civil rights.
She started her famous fairness calls
In 1848 at Seneca Falls.

Up 'til then no woman could vote.
Or own a home or banker's note.

Girls were told that they shouldn't dare
To be like boys. But that wasn't fair!

So, Stanton spoke, she wrote, and boldly led
The growing group of those who pled
For equal rights...that we later saw
Ruth Bader Ginsburg make the law.

Teachable Moment

Information:
Elizabeth Cady Stanton did not change the law in her lifetime. But she was one of the women leaders who started the long, slow effort to get girls and women treated more fairly.

In the past, girls and women weren't allowed to go to some schools that boys and men could go to. And girls weren't allowed to play on baseball, basketball, or other teams. They were told that boys and men were supposed to be the boss and do the leading. Women were told that they shouldn't expect to get all the jobs that men did. Even if they could get the same jobs, then women found they didn't get paid the same amount of money to do the same jobs that men did. That wasn't fair. That is changing.

Elizabeth Cady Stanton, Susan Anthony, and others laid the groundwork, so people like Ruth Bader Ginsburg later could go to the U.S. Supreme Court and guide women's rights into law. Ruth Bader Ginsburg studied hard, so she did well in school. She became a lawyer. She learned about the U.S. Constitution, which contains the rules under which we all must live. Ginsburg taught herself all about the rights that people were supposed to have. She then helped people who weren't being treated fairly get fair treatment — equal justice — under the law.

Questions:
1. Can people change other people's minds just by telling other people that they are wrong? No. You must persuade people. Stanton, Ginsburg, and others studied the Constitution and taught themselves about the laws. After they taught themselves, then they could explain to people why our country should use the laws to be fair to everyone. Sometimes they used stories about those who had been treated unfairly, to make people better understand and care about their ideas. Ruth Bader Ginsburg worked hard to be really good at explaining things, logically but nicely like Lincoln did, so other people would listen and could understand.

2. Which other people in this book taught themselves what they needed to know? [Franklin, Jefferson, Hamilton, Marshall, Sequoyah, Douglass, Lincoln, Edison, Tarbell, Roosevelt, Salk, King, and others.]

3. Is life now fair; is there now equal justice for everyone?

4. How have things changed over time?

Activities:
Discuss why it is not only fair but also smart policy to let everyone have an equal chance to go to school, to get jobs, and help rule our country, instead of only letting some favored people do so.

Thomas A. Edison
1877-1930

Thomas Edison made an electric light.
He worked and worked 'til he got it right.
His lab in Menlo Park
Lit what used to be dark.
Now all could see to play at night.

Edison found ways to better use
Motors and his electrical fuse.
His movies enlightened
And light bulbs brightened
The length of a day that people could use.

Teachable Moment

Information:
Thomas Edison tried thousands of different materials before he finally made a practical electric light bulb that worked. He kept trying and trying and didn't quit, even though the first many things that he tried didn't work.

Edison was substantially deaf, but he did not let that prevent him from inventing hundreds of useful things.

Edison built generators to send electrical power to whole neighborhoods. He also invented phonographs, movies, motors and generators, and many useful things.

Questions:
1. Edison once said that, "Genius is 1% inspiration and 99% perspiration." What do you think that means? Does it mean that only really smart people can do great things? No. He meant that success is less about being really smart and much more due to hard work. And success is due to not giving up or quitting, just because of failing the first few times.

2. Who do we know who could have used electric lights in order to write or read letters and books? Abigail Adams, who wrote by candle light, and every other person in this book who lived before Thomas Edison perfected his electric light bulb in 1879.

3. Just because you are hard of hearing, can't see well, or can't walk well, does that mean you shouldn't try? No. You can always be good at something, if you work, study, and practice a lot.

Activities:
Name all the things that we now can do because of electric lights?
Name all the things that we now can do because of electricity?

Sitting Bull
1831-1890

Chief Sitting Bull, a Lakota Sioux,
Hated being told what he had to do.
When people tried to take his land,
He took Crazy Horse into his band.

He dreamed of a battle late one night;
He dreamed about a great Army fight.
Then Colonel Custer's men arrived.
But, almost none of them survived.

Chief Sitting Bull was one of the last
To sadly see that his freedom had passed.
Like Chief Joseph and Geronimo
He gave up to his Army foe.

Like the Blackfoot, Crow, and Arapaho
He no longer could hunt the buffalo.
There was nothing left on the grassy sea.
And who remembers Wounded Knee?

Teachable Moment

Information:
As Americans moved to the west, many people tried to come into Sitting Bull's Lakota Sioux lands, to try to find gold. And other settlers tried to put fences around Sioux lands that those settlers didn't own. Sitting Bull, Crazy Horse, Rain-in-the-Face, Gall, Black Moon, Red Horse, and many other Native Americans became angry about this. So there were many fights, and many people died.

The most famous fight was called Custer's Last Stand, June 25, 1876, when Sitting Bull's men killed Colonel Custer, killed Custer's two soldier brothers, and killed almost all of Colonel Custer's other soldiers, too. Amazingly, Sitting Bull dreamed about this battle before it happened.

Joseph was chief of the Nez Perce. And Geronimo was chief of the Apache. They also eventually surrendered to the U.S. Army. Chief Joseph famously but sadly said, "From where the sun now stands, I will fight no more forever."

For centuries there had been millions of buffalo on the "grassy sea" of the western great plains. But soldiers killed so many buffalo, that there were few left for the Native Americans.

Soldiers also killed many Native Americans, including peaceful women and children at Sand Creek and Wounded Knee. Some people are still angry about this.

Questions:
1. Did our country treat Native Americans fairly?

2. Who lived in the United States first: The Spanish explorers? The Pilgrims and settlers who came from other parts of Europe? The slaves who came from Africa? Or the Native Americans, who we believe came from Asia across a land

President Theodore Roosevelt 1858-1919

Teddy Roosevelt was a sick and weak little boy,
But he learned to box; a bully fight he did enjoy.
He made his mind and body strong.
He fought cheaters; he righted wrong.

He saved America's beautiful lands:
Wild animal homes and redwood stands;
Crater Lake, and Grand Canyon rim.
We named our Teddy bears for him.

Teachable Moment

Information:

Theodore Roosevelt had severe asthma as a child. And he was weak and sickly. But he was determined to improve himself. He exercised to strengthen his body. And he read and studied many books to strengthen his mind.

When president, he fought people who cheated the public. Roosevelt used the courts to keep one person from owning all the country's oil and then unfairly making everyone else pay really high prices for it. He "busted trusts" that did this kind of cheating.

Roosevelt sent Great White Fleet navy ships around the world, to show other countries that we were now a strong nation that should be treated fairly. He painted our Navy ships white, instead of the usual gray color, to show that we were peaceful.

Roosevelt read many books. Even as president, he read a book every day. So, he knew a lot. He also wrote more than forty books: about the Navy, about places he explored, about the American West, and about the cowboys he lived with for awhile — people he called "Rough Riders."

Roosevelt got Congress to pass Antiquity Act laws allowing some of America's most beautiful lands to be saved as wild areas. So, no one could put up buildings and scare away the animals that lived there. Now we all can visit these beautiful places and can see the wild animals.

Yes, all our Teddy bears were named after Theodore "Teddy" Roosevelt.

Questions:

1. If you are weak, must you always stay weak? Or can you do something about it? What can you do to make your body strong? Or better in sports? Is it easy to do that? Must you keep practicing?

2. How did Teddy Roosevelt learn about things and make his mind strong? Did he expect his teachers to do all the work of teaching him everything?

Activities:

Bring or have on hand Teddy bears and talk about how people in Teddy Roosevelt's time named their Teddy bears for him. Discuss how a national park protects plants and forests and allows the animals to live in their own wild homes inside the park, instead of in cages in zoos.

Ida M. Tarbell
1857-1944

When news reporting was at its worst
Ida Tarbell was among the first
To carefully report the news.
Ida Tarbell wrote honest reviews.

While some raked muck and made attacks
Tarbell always tried to find the facts.
She read, she asked; she listened with care
And carefully wrote what was fair.

Ida Tarbell was an honest sleuth;
She always tried to tell the truth.
She knew that she always must
Tell the truth to earn our trust.

Teachable Moment

Information:
A sleuth [pronounced slooth] is a detective who tries to find out what happened.

More than one hundred years ago, people who wrote dishonest news were called "Muckrakers." Muck means dirty, muddy stuff. And Muckrakers meant dishonest writers would just rake up dirty muck about other people and write about it.

Ida Tarbell was not a Muckraker. She taught herself what was real and what was fake. And she then wrote the truth. She didn't make things up.

People sometimes now accuse each other of making up facts that aren't true. But then, people trusted Ida Tarbell, because they knew she told the truth.

Questions:
1. Should we believe everything we hear or read? Why not?

2. Do we believe people who have lied to us?

3. If we don't tell the truth to other people, will they believe us at first? Will they believe us the next time, or any other time, if they know that we don't tell the truth?

Activities:
Discuss how can we find out what is true. Sometimes this can be difficult. We could try to find out what happened by looking in a library or online ourselves. And by asking other honest people who know about it and who we know we can trust. And we can ask several different people to see if they all agree with each other about the subject. And, if some people disagree with us, we should keep an open mind and give them a chance to explain their reasons for not agreeing. We should listen to what they think, and then we should decide if they might be right or not.

Oliver Wendell Holmes Junior
1841-1935

Oliver Wendell Holmes was a Supreme Court judge;
He made the First Amendment budge.
He read and wrote books, and he liked to teach.
He taught us about freedom of speech.

He said it's wrong to cry, "Fire!" in a crowded space
But our ideas had rights in the marketplace.
He said that all could complain, and people could state
Their thoughts about rulers — even thoughts that we hate.

Teachable Moment

Information:
The First Amendment to the U.S. Constitution says, among other things, that people have a right to say what they think, even if it makes other people mad, as long as it doesn't actually hurt other people. Oliver Wendell Holmes said that you aren't allowed to yell, "Fire!" in a movie theater, because that could cause people to panic and trample each other when running to get out and would be dangerous. Importantly, Holmes said that we have the right to say that we don't like our president, our congress, our state and town leaders, or other ruling people who try to tell us what to do.

Justice Holmes said you can disagree with and say unpleasant things about our government — the people who rule us — without getting in trouble. He also said that people with bad ideas — even ideas that we might hate — have a right to speak about their ideas. He said that all ideas have a right to be heard and judged in the "marketplace" of ideas. The best response to bad ideas and bad speech is not to keep people from talking but rather the best response is better speech — to show why bad speech is bad. Do you know that other countries sometimes put people in jail just for talking; for complaining about their rulers? But Holmes said this should not happen in America. We can always complain about our rulers in our country.

Questions:
1. Do you think that we can say whatever we want about anyone? Even if what we say isn't true? Or gets someone else in trouble? No. You shouldn't say things that aren't true and that cause other people to lose their jobs or get hurt because of what you say.

2. Are the speech laws the same in all countries?

3. Are our own speech laws the same for what we can say about all people? No. We can say more about our rulers and "public figures" than we can say about other people.

4. Even if you are allowed to, is it always the right thing to say mean things about other people? Or is it smarter to be polite, if you want the other person to listen to what you say?

Activities:
Discuss what you think we should be able to say about other people or about what we believe. Look up whether the First Amendment allows you to say or write whatever you want to: About your rulers, About your neighbors, About your job or your boss at work, About other people you know. Look up "public figure" and what you may say about

Albert Einstein
1879-1955

Albert Einstein without his hat
Was very wildly haired.
But he figured out from where he sat
That energy, E, equals M C squared.

And that clocks slow down when things speed up
And that light bends with gravity.
He saw energy in a water cup.
And he called all this...Relativity.

Albert Einstein was really smart.
He warned, with calm aplomb
How tiny atoms could split apart.
And make a terrible atomic bomb.

Teachable Moment

Information:
Albert Einstein was one of the most intelligent people who ever lived. Einstein said that he did not always accept what other people thought as true. Instead, he decided himself whether it was true. He spent a lot of time just thinking about things.

Einstein figured out many of the ways in which our world works. He taught people to think differently about what time is, what space is, and how gravity works. His most famous equation was $E=mc^2$ that told us that huge amounts of energy were contained in matter.

Because of Einstein, we have GPS. We can calculate better paths for our rockets in space. And we understand the world around us much better than we ever did before.

Einstein warned President Franklin Roosevelt that bad people were trying to make a terrible atomic bomb and might use it against us, unless we built one first. So President Roosevelt told our scientists to start building an atomic bomb. Our country was the first to make atomic bombs.

Questions:
1. Must we believe everything, just because we read it or because another person told us that?

2. Are smart people, adults, and even teachers always right? Or can we try to find out what is true by ourselves? Was Einstein right every single time?

3. See how electrons surround an atom. [Atoms are much smaller than in the picture.] And how satellites revolve around our earth?

Activities:
Discuss how scientists think. If someone important tells a scientist what to think, does a scientist just automatically believe it? Or does a scientist first test to see if it is right? Discuss how a scientist is willing to change her mind, if new facts show that a previous belief is wrong. Discuss what scientists' discoveries now allow us to do and how science

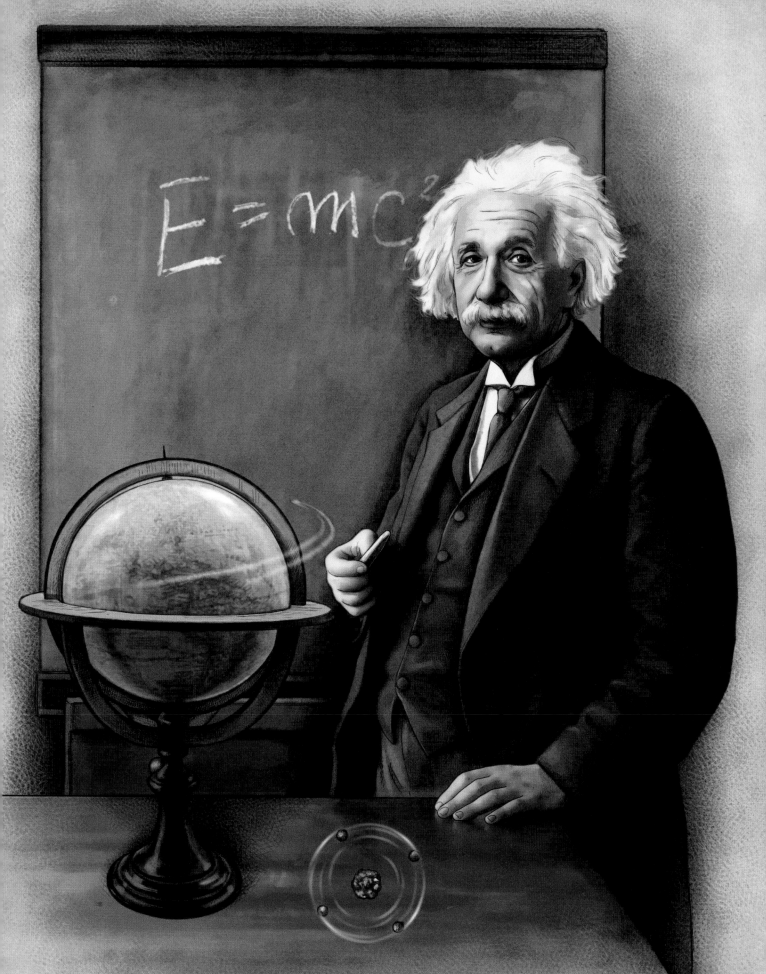

President Franklin Delano Roosevelt 1882-1945

Franklin Roosevelt couldn't walk.
But he could think, and he could talk.
Polio made him a disabled man.
But he said to himself: "I can!"

When banks lost our money, and dust storms raged
He gave hope to the poor and help to the aged.
He calmed our fears by radio session;
He got us through a great depression.

He didn't want a coming fight,
But he rallied our righteous might
So, when enemies bombed and torpedoed us too,
He led us to win World War Two.

Teachable Moment

Information:
Franklin Roosevelt was a cousin of Theodore Roosevelt. Franklin Roosevelt couldn't walk, because his legs didn't work due to the disease called polio. Polio viruses were tiny germs that killed the nerves that made muscles work. So, Roosevelt could not move his leg muscles and so he could barely walk and couldn't climb up stairs. Notice how Franklin Roosevelt had to use a wheelchair. And see the metal braces on each side of his shoes? Those braces went all the way above his knees. Those metal braces kept his legs from falling when he stood up. Note, next page, how Jonas Salk later invented a vaccine to keep polio from harming other people.

Many people lost all their money during the Great Depression, when banks ran out of money. And people living in Kansas, Oklahoma, Texas, and other nearby states suffered horrible dust storms. Dust even got through the closed doors and taped windows of people's houses, so many people inside were covered in dust. And some people breathed and coughed up lots of dust.

Roosevelt talked to the American people by radio. There was no TV or internet then. Many people felt that President Roosevelt cared about them and was doing his best to help. So, when unhappy people in other countries turned fascist, or voted for new, bad leaders, we didn't. An enemy surprise attack sank our navy ships and killed more than two thousand of our sailors at Pearl Harbor, Hawaii, on December 7, 1941. As a result, we entered and then won World War II.

Questions:
1. If we can't walk, run, or do some things as well as other people, should we just give up, and not try to do things?

2. Do you think that everyone can be good at something?

Activities:
Discuss what can we use and what we can do to help people who cannot walk well get to the same buildings, sidewalks, upstairs, and other places we all like to go?

46

Dr. Jonas Salk
1914-1995

Millions of children now can walk
Because of Dr. Jonas Salk.
Salk taught himself what he needed to know
About the dreaded virus — polio.

Salk invented a vaccination shot
So tiny polio germs could not
Cripple kids' legs and arms
Or cause other horrible harms.

Mommies and daddies used to fear
That polio germs were coming here.
Now millions of children are able to walk
Because of Dr. Jonas Salk.

Teachable Moment

Information:
Polio is a terrible disease caused by a tiny virus. A virus is so small that we cannot even see it. If a bad virus gets inside us, it can make us sick. A polio virus makes the nerves that control our muscles sick, so our leg or arm muscles won't work anymore. Franklin Roosevelt had polio and couldn't walk because of it.

Dr. Salk read and studied to teach himself all about the polio virus. He kept trying and didn't quit, until he learned how to make a vaccine that fought against polio. Dr. Salk, Dr. Sabin, and others made vaccinations that helped our bodies fight and kill polio germs.

People like Bill and Melinda Gates are gradually making sure that every child in the world gets vaccinated against polio. Someday, they may rid the Earth of this horrible disease.

Bad germs, like viruses and bacteria, used to infect and kill many babies and children before they could grow up. Many, many children used to die of infections and diseases. Eleven year-old Willie Lincoln died of typhoid when his father, Abraham Lincoln was president. Even grown-ups like Abigail Adams and Ann Rutledge died of diseases like typhoid. Now we give vaccination shots that help your body fight those bad germs. So now vaccinated babies and children almost never die because of germs infecting them.

Questions:
1. How did Dr. Salk learn about the polio virus?

2. How can anyone learn about something, if no teacher is nearby?

3. Can teachers teach us about everything? Or should we all learn how to teach ourselves?

4. Can you name other people who taught themselves what they wanted to know?

Activities:
Ask your doctor, physician's assistant, or nurse or look on the internet what diseases your shots protect you from. Do we get typhoid shots, so we don't die of typhoid like Abigail Adams, Ann Rutledge, and Willie Lincoln did? Ask your grandparents if they remember seeing anyone with polio from long ago. How did polio affect those people? Discuss what, besides vaccinations, we must do to stay in good health.

Rachel Carson
1907-1964

Rachel Carson made us see
How birds were killed by DDT.
She wrote a book that opened our eyes
To how we poisoned our beautiful skies
And woods and fields and rivers and sea.

She told us there was a Silent Spring
With very few songbirds left to sing.
She showed us how to fix all this
So never again those songs to miss.
Rachel Carson did a wonderful thing.

Teachable Moment

Information:
Rachel Carson wrote the book called Silent Spring. She explained what was happening and why it was wrong to poison our environment — the place in which we live.

She showed how certain poisons that people used to kill insects caused the birds that ate the insects to get the same poison that was inside the insects. And that the poison in the birds then caused them to lay bad eggs, with weak outer shells. Those bad egg shells would crack early and kill the baby birds before they were ready to hatch. So, there were fewer birds to sing their songs.

Now we don't use some of those poisons. So, birds' eggs are healthy again. And the birds are back singing to each other and to us.

Questions:
1. What would our country look like, if everyone were allowed to dump dirty garbage, or paint, or poisons, and junk everywhere?

2. There used to be millions of colorful butterflies. But now it's hard to find butterflies in our yards. Why do you think we no longer can see many butterflies?

3. Why is it so important that we all have clean water?

Activities:
Discuss how we can help protect our trees, birds, other animals, and waters.

Martin Luther King, Jr.
1929-1968

Reverend Martin Luther King
Did Gandhi's non-violent thing.
He saw racial hating
And got tired of waiting
So, he made freedom ring.

Martin Luther King
His words stand up and sing.
He pushed for civil rights
Without any fights
He made freedom ring.

Martin Luther King
He loved each living thing.
He said, "I have a dream"
Of justice as a mighty stream.
And he made freedom ring.

Teachable Moment

Information:
Mohandas (Mahatma) Gandhi was a famous man from the country called India. Gandhi wanted India to be free to be its own country. But Gandhi didn't like fighting. So, he helped free India without fighting. Later, Martin Luther King thought that Gandhi got freedom for his people in the right way. So, King helped people get treated more fairly, without having to fight or hurt other people to do so. King helped African American people gather and march — to politely ask for fair treatment — even as television showed other people being mean to them for doing so.

King was a very good writer and speaker. In other words, King was good at rhetoric. Like Abraham Lincoln, King learned to use rhetoric to make people care, and to make people remember the important things that he had to say. So King taught people all over the country how life was unfair for many African Americans.

King gave his most famous speech at the Lincoln Memorial, in Washington D.C. in 1963. That was called King's "I have a dream" speech. He stood near the famous statue of Abraham Lincoln. And he told the world how much more needed to be done to make life fairer for everyone.

Questions:
1. Remember Thomas Jefferson's 1776 Declaration of Independence phrase, "all men are created equal?" Did Martin Luther King help make Jefferson's "all men are created equal" declaration more true than it had been before? Who else in this book also did so?

2. Who else is pictured near Martin Luther King in this picture? Why were these other people also important?

Activities:
You can watch King's great "I have a dream" speech on You Tube. (For very small children, just watch the ending of

Neil Armstrong
1930-2012

Neil Armstrong studied and trained a lot.
He was our most famous astronaut.
He flew rocket planes with perfect grace.
He rode big rockets into outer space.

In nineteen hundred and sixty-nine
With awesome calm and a famous line
He landed the Eagle on Tranquility Base.
He was first on the Moon for the human race.

He said that he took one small step for a man.
He stepped on the moon as an American.
He took one giant leap for humanity.
He's the bravest person we'll ever see.

Teachable Moment

Information:
Before chosen to be an astronaut, Neil Armstrong was one of our best and bravest test pilots. Armstrong studied, learned, practiced a lot, and he practiced well, so he got to be good.

Armstrong always kept his head about him. He did not panic. He stayed calm, even when scary things happened and even when things got out of control. Tranquility Base was the place on the Moon where Neil Armstrong and Buzz Aldrin landed their moon rocket. Then Neil Armstrong became the first human being to get out of their space ship and walk on the moon.

Being an astronaut is dangerous. Rockets can blow up. And space ships can break apart or burn up while slamming into the air when coming back to Earth. Astronauts must be able to calmly talk and tell people on the ground what is happening, even when the astronauts are facing great danger. Astronauts are some of the bravest people in the world.

When you want to be good at something, you also must work at it and practice, again and again, just like Neil Armstrong did. If you study, learn, and then practice enough, you can usually be better at what you want to do than most other people

Questions:
1. Can you find the small part of this huge Saturn V rocket where the astronauts stayed? Note that the Apollo crew's space capsule was only a small part of the rocket.

2. If you want to be really good at something, what must you do?

Activities:
See Armstrong's space suit? Find out why he needed to wear a space suit and helmet when he was in space and on the moon? Get cardboard boxes and make your own small space capsule. Color them and put in some windows. See how little room the astronauts have when they go into space? Bring everything you need to stay in your space capsule for a long while: Food, water, electronic gadgets, etc. Was there gravity in space?

Afterward

It is common, in these contentious times, to pick out flaws in people's characters. And then to object to any recognition given them. One can, no doubt, find flaws in some of those depicted in this book. Different times produced different values and different behaviors. But each person here had some great qualities and achievements. This book emphasizes the positives of these great people. And the book is designed to let the reader select and focus upon those subjects desired.

As children mature, teach themselves, and think for themselves — as they should — they may reach somewhat different conclusions about our subjects. And some may prefer other subjects than those chosen here. But the author contends that we all should know something about this volume's great people — people who helped make our culture what it is. This book proposes to be a springboard toward such goals.

The book also emphasizes personal qualities that children can acquire: industry, diligence, practice, fairness, civility, and the profound importance of learning how to teach themselves — for the rest of their lives.

Those who hoped to see more diversity in this book are reminded of how multiple glass ceilings have hitherto impeded some who were capable of greatness. This book is written in the hope that such barriers will continue to recede. And in the hope that children to whom this book is read will be empowered and will commit to overcome any and all such impediments.

If you liked this book, please go to Amazon.com and give it a positive rating. I would also appreciate your feedback at **PhidacticP@gmail.com.**

Acknowledgements:

The author thanks Mechanicsburg Arch Street School fifth grade teacher, Clara Hewett, who inspired a lifelong love of history; Coronado middle school teacher, Kenneth Hantze, who made history and the U.S. Constitution even more interesting; Dartmouth Professor, Jere Daniell, for fascinating new insights and for teaching how to write about it; and Anne Pennington, for her numerous suggested — and often initially resisted — improvements. Many thanks also to Conrad Cutcliffe, Ashley Cutler, Jared Inselmann, colleagues at the Westerly Library Adult Writers' Workshop, Patricia Schwartz, Jenny Sykes, Lila Thorne, and David Willetts for their helpful suggestions.

And my wife, Ronnie, for her help with this book, and for keeping me alive and enchanted during its writing.

About

The Author:

Philo Willetts graduated from Dartmouth College with a degree in history. He wrote these illustrated verses to prime young people's knowledge about some great Americans and their fascinating times. And to instill into our children some of the positive qualities of these distinguished people.

He can be reached at PhidacticP@gmail.com

The Illustrator:

Iva Sasheva, a professional freelance artist and writer, holds a master's degree in Fine Arts, and has had a number of exhibitions in Europe. She has worked as a storyboard artist for many feature films and hundreds of commercials. She has collaborated with authors in the creation of graphic novels, children's books, and works of literary fiction. She also writes and illustrates short stories.

Iva Sasheva can be reached at www.ivasasheva.com

The Designer:

Stephen Schwartz has a bachelor's degree from Fordham University in Visual Arts, specializing in graphic design. He has extensive international experience designing for clients in digital and print spaces across the USA, Europe and the United Kingdom.

He can be reached at: www.thisissteveschwartz.com

Made in the USA
Middletown, DE
23 August 2019